TRAITS AND HEREDITY

JOSEPH MIDTHUN   SAMUEL HITI

BUILDING
BLOCKS

SCIENCE

I0111447

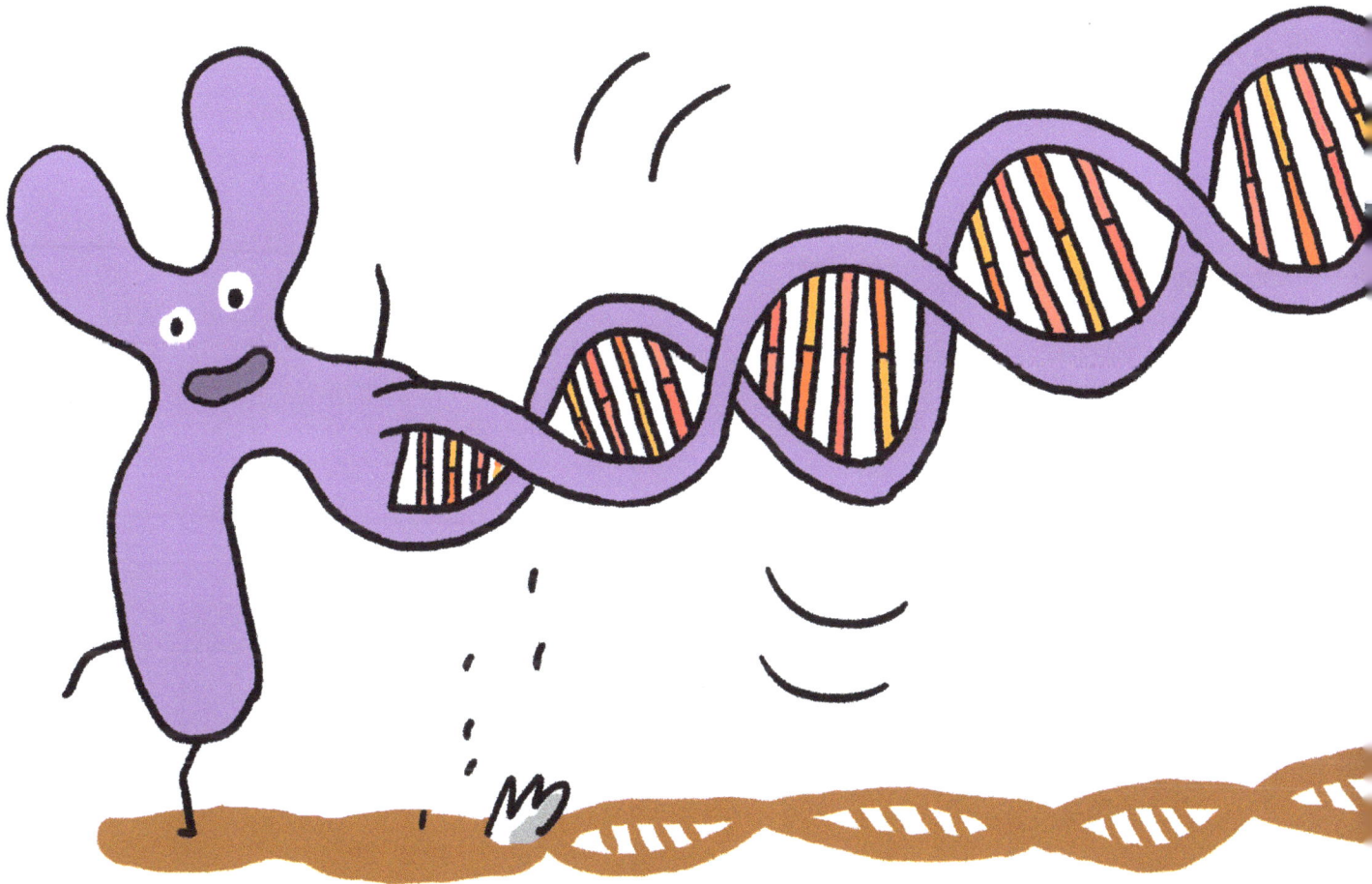

WORLD
BOOK

www.worldbook.com

World Book, Inc.
180 North LaSalle Street
Suite 900
Chicago, Illinois 60601
USA

For information about other World Book publications,
visit our website at www.worldbook.com
or call 1-800-WORLDBK (967-5325).
For information about sales to schools and libraries,
call 1-800-975-3250 (United States),
or 1-800-837-5365 (Canada).

Building Blocks of Science:
  Traits and Heredity
ISBN: 978-0-7166-7883-0 (trade, hc.)
ISBN: 978-0-7166-7891-5 (pbk.)
ISBN: 978-0-7166-2966-5 (e-book, EPUB3)

Acknowledgments:
Created by Samuel Hiti and Joseph Midthun
Art by Samuel Hiti
Text by Joseph Midthun
Special thanks to Syril McNally

TABLE OF CONTENTS

There is a glossary on page 30. Terms defined in the glossary are in type **that looks like this** on their first appearance.

Cells are tiny **organisms** that work together to make up all living things.

You are made up of **cells.**

You can think of cells as the building blocks of life!

But, how do cells build a person or a plant?

Chemicals and proteins are not organisms, but when they are brought together in a specific order inside the cell, they make up tiny structures called **genes.**

Genes are made of chains of proteins like deoxyribonucleic acid, or—

—DNA!

The special combination of DNA in your genes can be understood—

—and even copied by the cell.

Plop

In fact, these genes have special instructions that control how a living thing grows and inherits, or receives, its parents' characteristics, or **traits!**

WHAT ARE TRAITS?

There are many things known as characteristics that make up your appearance.

These characteristics are examples of traits.

A trait is something that not all living things of a particular type have in common.

A trait can be any characteristic of a living thing.

Eye color, hair color, height, and weight can all vary and are controlled by the tiny genes inside of cells.

For instance, a lot of animals have ears.

So, having ears is not considered a trait.

But not every ear is shaped the same way.

That means the shape of an ear is a trait.

Your specific combination of traits makes you who you are.

And although you share some traits with your parents, you are unique—

—different from everyone else.

INHERITANCE

Heredity is the passing on of biological characteristics from one generation to the next.

You get many of your traits through heredity.

The process of heredity occurs among all living things—animals, plants, and even such microscopic organisms as bacteria.

plip

When a trait is passed down from parent to child, it is inherited.

Plop

Inheritance forms a continuous chain of traits that run in families.

Heredity is the reason that offspring often look like their parents.

Your parents inherited their traits from their parents.

And you inherit many traits from your parents.

You may have inherited the shape of your nose from your mother.

Or you may have inherited your father's hair color.

In other animals, eye color, fur color and texture, and beak shape are examples of inherited traits.

Flower color, plant height, and leaf shape are some of the inherited traits of plants.

TRAITS AND GENES

Inside of a cell, genes are made up of DNA.

DNA forms long, threadlike patterns called **chromosomes.**

So, genes are carried inside of these chromosomes.

These chromosomes, and the genes inside, have instructions that control how cells grow and develop into a living organism.

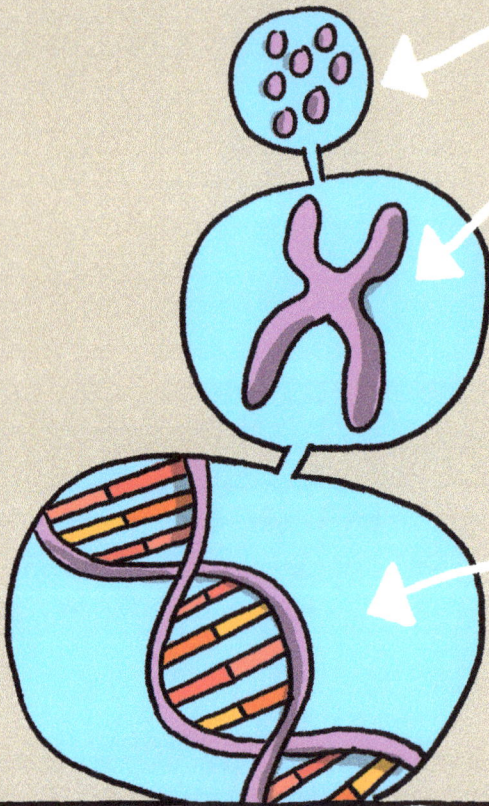

Because of the instructions in its genes, a tiger cub will grow up to look like its mother and father.

A seed from a maple tree will grow to become another maple tree.

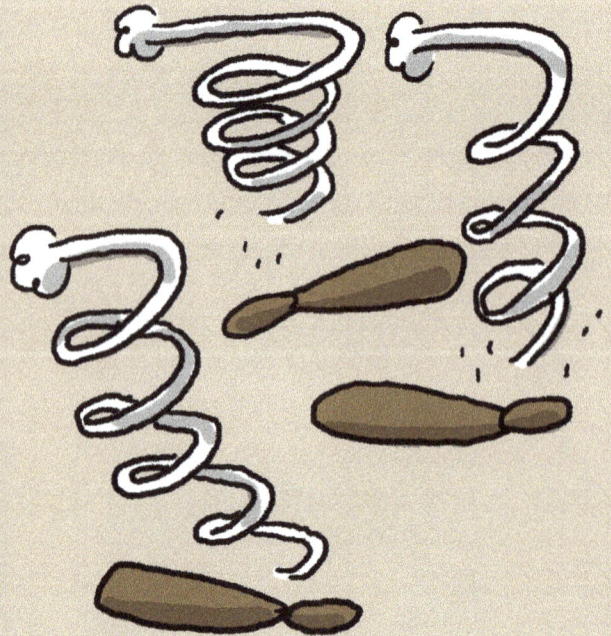

Genes are like blueprints for building a house.

But instead of walls and windows, they carry the plans for building cells, tissues, organs, and...

...the instructions for making the thousands of different sizes and shapes of body parts— or your traits!

Some traits are affected by a single gene alone.

Other traits are affected by many genes working together.

HOP

You have the same number of genes as every other human being.

Plop

But the instructions on the genes are different from one person to the next.

Lick
Lick
Lick

Milk

GENES AND REPRODUCTION

Reproduction is the process by which living things create more of their own kind.

The passing of genes from parent to **offspring** is an important part of reproduction.

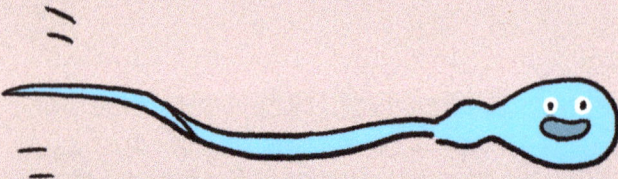

Genes are inherited by offspring from parents through reproduction.

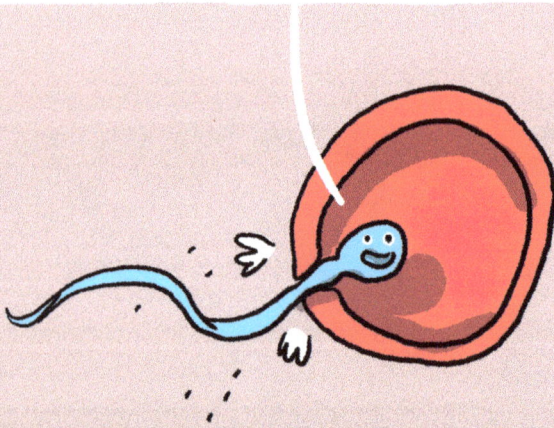

There are two general types of reproduction, asexual and sexual.

In **asexual reproduction**, all the offspring's genes come from a single parent.

When this worm reproduces asexually, its body divides into two sections.

One has the head.

The other has the tail.

Each section grows the parts that are missing and becomes a new worm.

In this type of reproduction, each offspring has the same set of genes as its parent.

In plants, **vegetative propagation** is a form of asexual reproduction that happens when a leaf, runner, or other part forms a new plant.

ROOTS

The runner of this strawberry plant carries an identical copy of the parent plant's genes.

RUNNER

If the runner forms new roots, it uses the parent plant's genes to develop into a new plant!

NEW ROOTS

Sexual reproduction generally involves two parents, each giving half of the chromosomes carrying genes to the offspring.

MALE

FEMALE

Sexual reproduction starts with the production of specialized sex cells called **gametes.**

SPERM

EGG

Sperm cells, **egg** cells, and plant **pollen** grains are all gametes.

OFFSPRING

...and the egg cell has only half of the gene pairs from the mother.

A sperm cell contains only half of the father's gene pairs...

In human beings, sperm and egg cells have 23 chromosomes each.

When an egg cell and a sperm cell unite through a process called **fertilization,** they combine and create the full number of chromosomes.

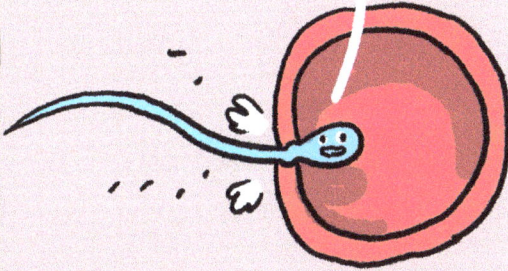

The resulting cell, known as a fertilized egg, has 46 chromosomes, or 23 pairs.

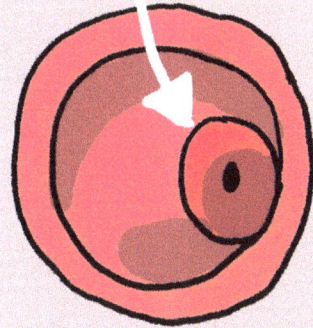

One chromosome of each pair comes from the mother's egg, and the other from the father's sperm.

This is how the offspring gets one half of its gene pairs from each parent.

After the egg is fertilized, it follows the chromosome's instructions and begins dividing into more cells to create an offspring.

The offspring then develops the traits inherited from both of its parents.

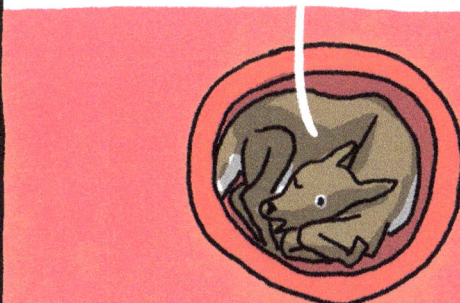

GENES AND VARIATION

You have thousands of genes.

Those genes can come in many varieties.

Variation in genes is what makes each person different from everyone else!

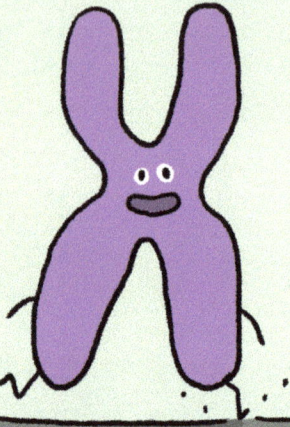

Most genes come in pairs.

Hi.

Each pair of genes is held in a pair of matching chromosomes, with one copy of a gene in each chromosome.

Do you have any 8's?

Nope. Go fish!

Different forms of the same gene are called **alleles**.

Some alleles are dominant, and others are recessive.

wack

HEY!

A **dominant allele** hides the effects of its recessive partner.

In other words, the dominant allele is expressed, or seen, and the recessive allele is not.

OOF!

swoop

catch

A trait from a **recessive allele** is seen only in an organism that has two recessive alleles for that one trait.

Some hereditary traits are determined by a single pair of genes.

And other traits are controlled by many pairs of genes.

Tens or hundreds of pairs of genes direct the inheritance of such traits as height, weight, and intelligence.

In the mid-1800's, scientist and monk Gregor Mendel performed a now-famous experiment that crossed, or mated, a purple flower pea plant with a white flower pea plant.

The first **generation** of offspring had plants with all purple flowers.

After Mendel crossed the plants again, he saw the trait for white flowers in the second generation.

Even though the first-generation plant did not have any white flowers, it was a **carrier,** meaning it still carried the gene for the trait of white flowers.

A carrier is an organism that carries and transfers a recessive gene, but does not show that trait physically.

PARENT PLANTS

PP   PP

FIRST GENERATION

Pp   Pp   Pp   Pp

SECOND GENERATION

PP   Pp   Pp   PP

The white flower trait in the first generation had been hidden by the trait for purple flowers.

Mendel discovered that in pea plants the allele that produces purple flowers (symbolized by P) is dominant over the one that forms white flowers (p).

Pea plants that have two dominant alleles for purple flowers (PP) or one allele for purple flowers and one for white flowers (Pp) will have purple flowers.

Only those plants with two recessive alleles (pp) will have white flowers.

Mendel's discovery helps us to understand how all of an organism's traits are passed from one generation to the next.

HYBRIDS

In the wild, hybrids occur naturally.

A **hybrid** is the offspring of parents of different breeds, varieties, or species.

However, the term hybrid is most often used when talking about plants bred by human beings.

Some scientists and farmers develop hybrids to improve the quality and number of crops.

Plants are selected for hybrid production because they have traits that growers want to pass on to the next generation of plants.

One variety of corn may resist disease better than another variety does.

But the second variety may be hardier in cold weather than the first.

Plop

By crossing the two varieties, growers can obtain hybrid seeds.

These seeds develop into hybrid plants that have the desired traits of both parents.

Hybrid plant seeds can be crossed again to make a different plant!

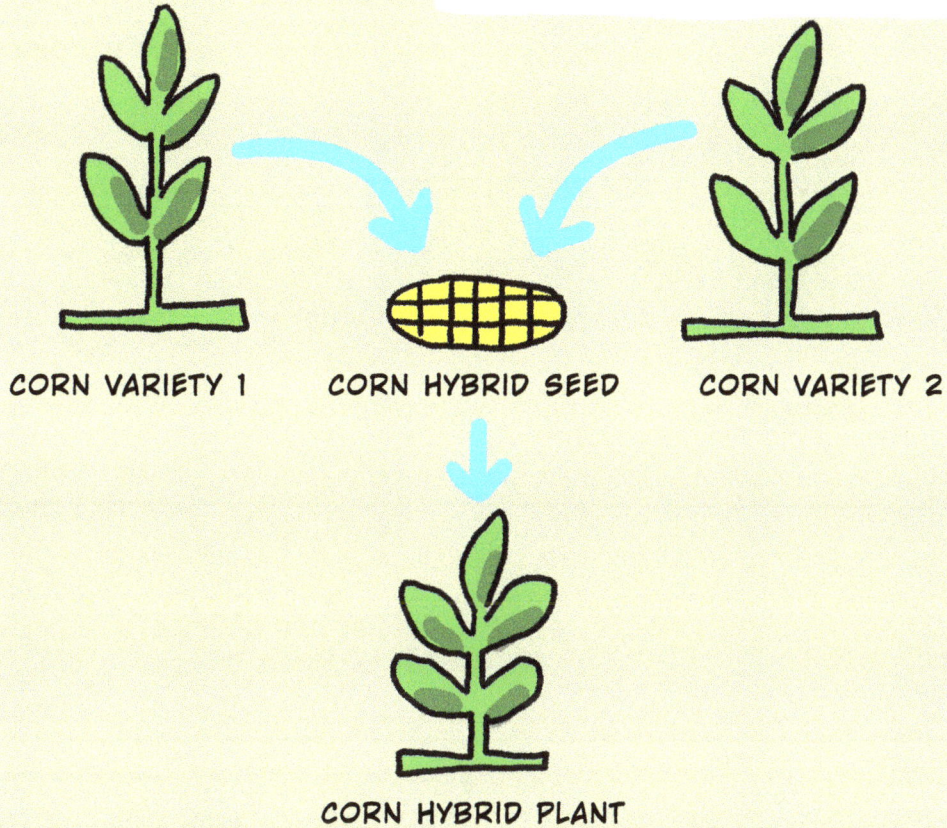

CORN VARIETY 1   CORN HYBRID SEED   CORN VARIETY 2

CORN HYBRID PLANT

People also make hybrid animal livestock by mating different breeds, called **crossbreeding.**

Cattle crossbreeds are one of the most common animal hybrids worldwide because they can yield a leaner meat to eat than do other cattle.

MUTATION

Mutation is a permanent change in the amount, structure, or pattern of the DNA in an organism's cells.

Mutations in the DNA can be passed on in the chromosomes from a parent to its offspring.

Many mutations affect entire chromosomes—

NORMAL CELL   MUTATED CELLS

—and the genes carried inside—

—which can change an organism's traits.

In some cases, an organism has too many or too few chromosomes.

People with Down syndrome have an extra copy of chromosome 21, one of the 23 pairs of chromosomes.

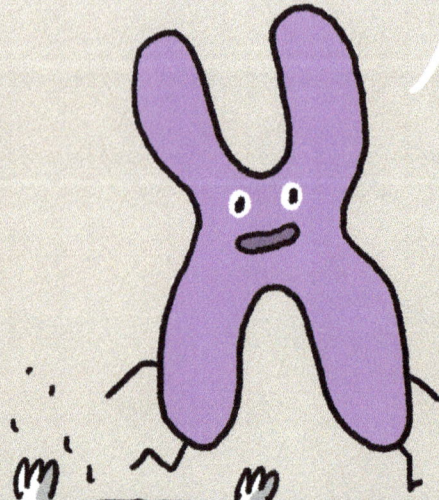

Sometimes the structure of a chromosome is abnormal.

A mutation called translocation occurs when part of one chromosome breaks off and attaches to another.

Other mutations are caused by changes in an organism's environment, such as **pollution.**

Many species of frogs have been found with mutations to their legs.

Pollution in the environment can enter animals' bodies and affect cell development.

As a result, the frog's early physical development can be changed.

HOP

ENVIRONMENTAL INFLUENCES

Genes have powerful effects, but they do not control all of life.

Most characteristics come from a combination of both heredity and environment.

Not all traits come from genes.

You also have traits that are due to **nurture**, or characteristics that are influenced by the world around you.

The ability to speak is inherited through genes.

But, you learn your language from other people around you.

Hey, what's up?

Oh, just learning stuff.

Traits learned from your surroundings, like your favorite foods and the activities you enjoy, can change over time.

munch

munch

And, because a gene gives you the ability to develop a trait...

...how this trait is developed over time depends partly on the interaction of that gene with other genes (nature) and partly on your environment (nurture).

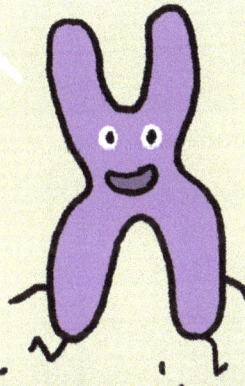

Thanks to both your genes and your surroundings, you can adapt!

WOO-HOO!

You are able to learn to like a food that you didn't like before!

crunch

Scientists debate the connection between heredity and environment in shaping a person's physical appearance and behavior.

Nurture.

NATURE!

This debate is often called the question of nature versus nurture—

—that is, heredity versus environment!

To try to understand the impact of both genes and the environment on a person, scientists studied identical twins, who have the exact same genes.

Hmm.

These studies show that identical twins raised apart in two different environments differ more in their characteristics than identical twins who were raised together.

As a result, scientists know that both heredity and environment play important roles in what an individual's ultimate appearance and behaviors will be.

Scientists have also started to uncover the causes of hereditary diseases, like heart disease, and are developing ways to treat them.

By looking at your specific genes, you can discover how to use your environment to keep yourself healthy.

You can find out what foods to eat or activities to avoid to help prevent sickness.

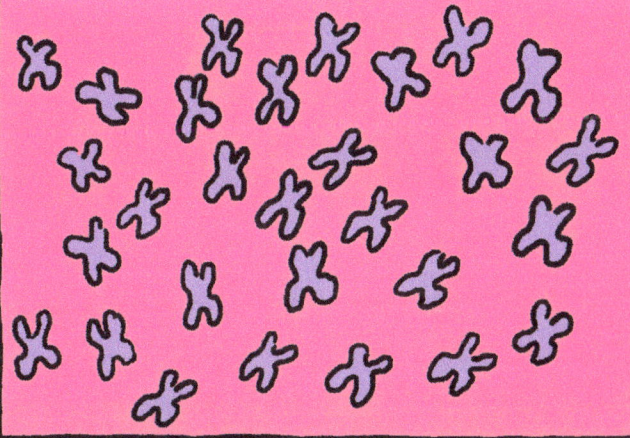

If you pass those traits down to your offspring...

...then your environment has had a hand in affecting your offspring's heredity!

YOUR TRAITS

Individual members of any species can differ widely from one another in their genetic makeup and, therefore, in their traits.

While you may look like your parents, you are not an exact duplicate of either of them...

...rather, a blend of both!

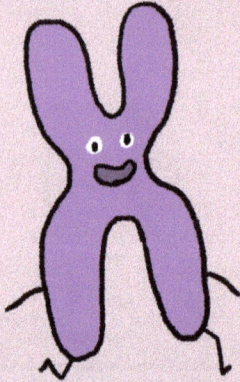

Just take a moment to think about what an amazing and complex organism you are.

From the DNA inside your cells' chromosomes to the environment you are a part of —

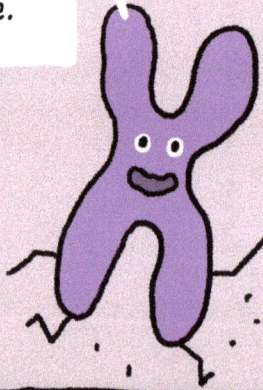

— there is only one you!

And, not only can your traits be affected by your environment...

...you can, and do, affect the traits of other organisms as well.

Every day, our understanding of traits and heredity is growing and changing.

The question is—

—will you control your traits?

Or, will your traits control you?

GLOSSARY

allele different forms of the same gene.

asexual reproduction the process by which an organism produces an offspring without sperm cells or egg cells.

carrier an organism that has and transfers a recessive gene, but does not show that trait physically.

cell the basic unit of all living things.

chromosomes tiny threadlike strands that carry genes.

crossbreeding mating different breeds of livestock animals.

DNA the chainlike structures found in cells that direct cell formation and growth.

dominant allele a form of a gene expressed as a trait that hides the effect of the recessive allele.

egg the female reproductive cell.

fertilization the process by which a male sperm cell and a female egg cell join together.

generation a group of organisms that live during the same time period.

gametes an organism's sex cells.

genes the part within a cell that determines an organism's traits.

heredity the process by which traits are passed down from parents to offspring.

hybrid the offspring of parents of different breeds, varieties, or species.

inheritance the process of receiving a trait that is passed down from parent to child.

mutation a permanent change in the DNA and chromosomes in an organism's cells.

nurture the influence on development by the environment.

offspring the young of an organism.

organism any living thing.

pollen a fine, yellowish powder formed in a flower that fertilizes a plant's egg.

pollution harmful substances made by humans that damage the environment.

recessive allele a form of a gene that is only expressed as a trait when the dominant allele is not present.

reproduction the way living things make more of their own kind.

sexual reproduction the process by which organisms produce offspring with sperm cells and egg cells.

sperm the male reproductive cell.

trait a physical or behavioral characteristic.

variation the difference in characteristics within a group.

vegetative propagation a form of asexual reproduction in plants.

FIND OUT MORE

Books

Change It! Solids, Liquids, Gases and Genetics
by Lynette Brent Sandvold
(Marshall Cavendish Benchmark, 2010)

Genetics: Investigating the Function of Genes and the Science of Heredity
by Trevor Day
(Rosen Central, 2013)

Inheritance and Reproduction
by Jen Green
(Capstone Heinemann Library, 2014)

The Manga Guide to Biochemistry
by Takemura, Masaharu, and Kikuyar
(No Starch Press, 2011)

Projects in Genetics
by Claire O'Neal
(Mitchell Lane, 2011)

Traits and Attributes
by Natalie Hyde
(Crabtree, 2010)

You Can't Wear These Genes
by Shirley Duke
(Rourke, 2011)

Websites

BBC Bitesize Science: DNA Activity
http://www.bbc.co.uk/schools
/gcsebitesize/science/add_edexcel
/cells/dnaact.shtml
Find out why your DNA is so important and how it controls your growth and development in this narrated activity.

BBC Bitesize Science: Genes
http://www.bbc.co.uk/schools
/gcsebitesize/science/21c/genes
/genesrev1.shtml
Read about your genes and then complete an animated instructional video and a multiple-choice test.

BBC Bitesize Science: Inheritance
http://www.bbc.co.uk/schools
/gcsebitesize/science/21c/genes
/inheritancerev1.shtml
Human reproduction and inheritance are examined in a short unit, complete with diagrams and boldface key terms.

Centre of the Cell: All About Cells
http://www.centreofthecell.org
/centre/?page_id=1&ks=2
Take an in-depth look at animal cells and examine the life cycle inside!

Centre of the Cell: Games and Interactives
http://www.centreofthecell.org/games/
Select a topic to play a clickable game or explore a 3D cell model to learn more about their function in your body.

DNA Learning Center: Code
http://www.dnai.org/a/index.html
Make your way through this comprehensive lesson to learn about the problem, players, puzzle, and resolution of your DNA!

Nobelprize.org – DNA: The Double Helix
http://www.nobelprize.org/educational
/medicine/dna_double_helix/
Play The Double Helix game to determine the DNA of three different organisms—and learn about genetics in the process.

Nova Online: Journey into DNA
http://www.pbs.org/wgbh/nova/genome
/dna.html#
Explore chromosomes up close as you travel into the tiny world of DNA.

INDEX

www.ingramcontent.com/pod-product-compliance
Lightning Source LLC
LaVergne TN
LVHW070840080426
835513LV00023B/2422